DESCARTES IN 90 MINUTES

Descartes
IN 90 MINUTES

Paul Strathern

IVAN R. DEE
CHICAGO

Library of Congress Cataloging-in-Publication Data:
Strathern, Paul, 1940–
    Descartes in 90 minutes / Paul Strathern.
      p.   cm. — (Philosophers in 90 minutes)
    Includes bibliographical references and index.
    ISBN 1-56663-128-9 (cloth : alk. paper). —
    ISBN 1-56663-129-7 (paper : alk. paper)
    1. Descartes, René, 1596–1650. I. Title. II. Series.
B1875.S87   1996
194—dc20   96-24946

Contents

DESCARTES IN 90 MINUTES

Introduction

By the end of the sixteenth century, philosophy had stopped. It was Descartes who started it up again.

Philosophy had begun for the first time in the sixth century B.C. in ancient Greece. Two centuries later it entered a golden era with Socrates, Plato, and Aristotle. Then, for nearly two thousand years, nothing happened. At least, nothing original happened.

Nonetheless several distinguished philosophers appeared during this period. The third-century Alexandrian Plotinus refined Plato's philosophy, in the process creating Neoplatonism. St. Augustine of Hippo then refined Neo-platonism to the point where it was acceptable to Christian theology. The Islamic scholar Averroës refined parts of Aristotle's philosophy, and Thomas Aquinas in turn rendered these acceptable to Christian theology. All four of these disparate figures advanced the course of philosophy, but not one of them produced an entirely new philosophy of his own. Their work was essentially exegesis, commentary, and elaboration of the philosophy of Plato and Aristotle. In this way these two pagan philosophers (and their pagan philosophies) became pillars of the Christian church. This intellectual conjuring trick was the main foundation of Scholasticism, the name given to philosophical activity during the Middle Ages. Scholasticism was the philosophy of the church and prided itself on its lack of originality. New philosophical ideas resulted only in heresy, the Inquisition, and burning at the stake. The ideas of Plato and Aristotle gradually became buried beneath layers of religiously correct Christian commentary, and philosophy dried up.

By the mid-fifteenth century this moribund stage had been reached in almost all fields of intellectual endeavor. The church reigned supreme throughout the medieval world. But already the first cracks were beginning to appear in this vast edifice of intellectual certainty. Ironically the main source of these cracks was the same classical world that had produced Plato and Aristotle. Much learning that had been lost or forgotten during the Dark Ages now began coming to light, inspiring a renaissance (or rebirth) of human knowledge.

The Renaissance brought with it a new humanistic outlook. This was followed by the Reformation, which ended the hegemony of the church. Yet more than a hundred years after these developments had transformed Europe, philosophy remained stuck in the bog of Scholasticism. This came to an end only with the arrival of Descartes, who produced a philosophy fit for the new era. In no time this spread through Europe and even achieved the ultimate accolade of being named after its founder: Cartesianism.

Descartes's Life and Works

Descartes never did a stroke of useful work in his life. At various times he described himself as a soldier, a mathematician, a thinker, and a gentleman. The last comes closest to describing his attitude toward life as well as his social status. His youthful inclination to a life of leisurely ease soon settled into a routine. He lived on his private income, rose at noon, and traveled when he felt like it. Such was his life—no dramas, no wives, no great public success (or failure). Yet Descartes was indisputably the most original philosopher to appear in the fifteen centuries following the death of Aristotle.

By the time Descartes arrived on the scene the Renaissance had brought a new humanistic outlook to Europe, and the Reformation had ended the hegemony of the Catholic church. Yet it remained for Descartes to launch the modern age of philosophy. From this period on, the primacy of the individual and the analysis of human consciousness became fundamental to philosophy, a focus that has only recently been superseded by the primacy of the dictionary and analysis of its contents.

René Descartes was born March 31, 1596, in the small town of La Haye, in the Creuse Valley thirty miles south of Tours, France. This spot has now been renamed Descartes, and if you visit it you can still see the house where he was born and the twelfth-century church of St. Georges where he was baptized.

René was the fourth child, and his mother was to die in childbirth the following year. His father Joachim was a judge in the High Court of Brittany. This met at Rennes, 140 miles away, which meant that Joachim was at home for less than half the year. He soon remarried, and René was brought up in the house of a grandmother. Here his main attachment was to his nurse, for whom he retained the fondest regard. He was to pay for her upkeep until the day she died.

Descartes spent a solitary childhood, accentuated by his sickly nature, and he quickly learned to do without company. From his early years he is known to have been introspective and reserved: a wan-faced child with thick curly black hair and large shadow-ringed eyes, wandering through the orchard in his black coat and knee breeches, a black wide-brimmed hat on his head and a long woolen scarf wound round his neck.

At the age of ten he was sent as a boarder to the Jesuit College that had recently opened in La Flèche. This school was intended for the education of the local gentry, who before this had often dispensed with such matters in favor of hunting, hawking, and halfhearted home homiletics. The rector of the college was a friend of the Descartes family, so the frail young René was given a room of his own and allowed to get up when he pleased. As with most who are permit-

13

ted such a privilege, this meant that Descartes rose around noon, a habit he strictly adhered to for the rest of his life. While the other pupils were being browbeaten by vicious and conceited Jesuits versed in the intricacies of Scholasticism, the intelligent young Descartes was thus able to absorb his learning in a more relaxed atmosphere, rising in time for luncheon followed by the riding, fencing, and flute-playing lessons that occupied the afternoon. By the time he came to leave, it was apparent that Descartes had learned far more than anyone else in the school, and his health appears to have completely recovered (apart from a lingering hypochondria, which he carefully nursed throughout his remarkably healthy life).

Yet despite carrying off all the prizes, Descartes retained a deep ambivalence toward his education. It seemed to him to be largely rubbish: rehashed Aristotle encrusted with centuries of interpretations; the stifling theology of Aquinas which had answers for everything but answered nothing; a morass of metaphysics. Nothing he learned appeared to have any certainty

14

whatsoever, apart from mathematics. And in a life devoid of the certainties of home, family, and meaningful social contact, Descartes craved certainty in the only realm in which he felt at home: the intellect. He left school disappointed. Like Socrates before him, he was convinced he knew nothing. Even mathematics was only capable of providing impersonal certainty. The only other certainty he knew was God.

When Descartes left La Flèche at eighteen, his father sent him to study law at the University of Poitiers. Joachim Descartes intended René to take up a respected position in the legal profession, just as his elder brother had done. In those days such positions were filled largely by nepotism, a system that succeeded in producing approximately the same percentage of ludicrous and inadequate judges as today. But after spending two years studying the law, Descartes decided he had had enough of it. By this time he had come into possession of a number of small rural properties inherited from his mother. These gave him a modest income, enough to live as he pleased. So he decided to set off for Paris "to pursue his thoughts." Judge Joachim was not pleased—the Descarteses were gentlemen and weren't expected to spend their time thinking. But there was nothing he could do about it: his son was now a free man.

After two years Descartes tired of his well-heeled bachelor existence in Paris. Despite devoting himself to a wide range of studies and composing a number of rather dilettantish treatises, he was becoming more and more involved in the social life of the capital, which he found utterly tedious. He withdrew to a quiet address in the Faubourg St. Germain, where no one went visiting, and lived in seclusion while pursuing his thoughts in peace.

This was to be Descartes's favored way of life throughout the rest of his years. Yet after settling down for a few months, he suddenly bolted. He seems to have been driven by two finely balanced obsessions: solitude and travel. Never having felt close to his fellow men, he had no wish to live in their company. And never having had a real home, he felt no desire to create one for himself. He was forever restless and solitary.

This makes Descartes's next move seem all the more extraordinary: he decided to join the army. In 1618 he went to Holland and signed on as an unpaid officer in the army of the Prince of Orange. The prince's Protestant army was preparing to defend the United Provinces of the Netherlands against the Catholic Spanish, who sought to retake their former colony. What the Dutch made of this aloof Catholic gentleman with no military experience, who professed to have done a bit of fencing and riding at school, is difficult to judge. At the time Descartes spoke no Dutch and stuck resolutely to his routine of rising at noon. Perhaps they just didn't notice him as he sat in his tent composing a treatise on music or some such. (Nowadays he would presumably be accused of being a spy; but in those days the military appear to have correctly gauged the importance of spies and were willing to sign on any recruits, regardless of nationality, allegiance, or even willingness to participate in military routine.)

We do know that Descartes found himself bored by life in the army; in his view there was "too much idleness and dissipation." Does this mean there were officers who arose even later than he did?

One afternoon, while strolling through the streets of Breda, Descartes noticed a poster being stuck up on a wall. In the manner of the time it outlined an unsolved mathematical problem and challenged all comers to solve it. Descartes didn't quite understand the instructions (they were, after all, in Dutch). He turned to the Dutch gentleman standing beside him and asked if he could kindly translate. The Dutchman was unimpressed by this ignorant young French officer. He replied that he would translate the poster only if the Frenchman were willing to try to solve the problem and bring him his solution. The following afternoon the young French officer arrived at the Dutchman's house, where to the Dutchman's surprise he found that the officer had not only solved the problem but had done so in exceptionally brilliant fashion.

According to Descartes's first biographer, Baillet, this was how Descartes met Isaac Beeckman, the renowned Dutch philosopher and

18

mathematician. The two were to remain close friends, corresponding regularly for the next two decades (with a few brief interruptions when they disagreed). "I was asleep until you wakened me," Descartes was to write to Beeckman. It was he who revived Descartes's interest in mathematics and philosophy, which had lain dormant since he had left La Flèche.

After a year or so in the Dutch army, Descartes set off on a summer tour of Germany and the Baltic. He then decided to try another spell of army life and journeyed to the small town of Neuburg in southern Germany, where the army of Maximilian Duke of Bavaria was camped in its winter quarters on the upper reaches of the Danube. Army life here appears to have been as strenuous as ever for Descartes, who describes how he took up residence in fine warm quarters, persisted in his habit of sleeping ten hours a night and rising at noon, and spent his waking hours "communing with my own thoughts."

The political situation in Europe was now becoming serious, though it's difficult to deduce this from Descartes's attitude. The Bavarians had gone to war against Frederick V, the elector palatinate and Protestant king of Bohemia. The entire continent was rapidly sliding into the long and disastrous conflict that came to be known as the Thirty Years War. This war, with its ever-changing fortunes affecting countries from Sweden to Italy, was to continue until virtually the end of Descartes's life, leaving large areas of Europe, especially in Germany, devastated and deserted. Yet the effect of this war on Descartes, even when he was in the army, appears to have been minimal. Still, one can't help suspecting that this persistent background of political uncertainty, together with Descartes's own psychological uncertainties, somehow contributed to the deep internal need for certainty that was to characterize his entire philosophy.

Meanwhile the Bavarian winter set in, and soon the snow lay round about deep and crisp and even. Descartes found it so cold he claims that he took to living in a stove—a subject of much debate. Some claim that Descartes really meant a well-heated room, others that he meant something more like a sauna. But Descartes uses the French word *poele*, which unquestionably means a stove.

One day while sitting in his stove, Descartes had a vision. It's not clear precisely what he saw under these rather steamed-up circumstances, but it seems that this vision contained a mathematical picture of the world. This convinced Descartes that the workings of the entire universe could be discovered by the application of some universal mathematical science. That night when Descartes went to sleep he had three vivid dreams. In the first he found himself struggling against an overpowering wind, trying to make his way down the street toward the church at his old college in La Flèche. At one point he turns to greet someone, and the wind flings him against the church wall. Then, from the middle of the courtyard, someone calls to him that a friend of his has a melon which he wants to give him.

In the next dream Descartes is overcome with terror and hears "a noise like a crack of lightning," after which the darkness of his room is filled with a myriad of sparks. The last dream is less clear: in the course of this he sees a dictionary and a book of poetry on his desk. This is followed by a number of the usual inconsequential and highly symbolic happenings that never fail to delight the dreamer and bore his listener. Descartes then decides (in his dream) to interpret these happenings. This might have given us a deep insight into Descartes's understanding of himself, but unfortunately his biographer Baillet becomes rather garbled at this point.

The events of that winter day and the following night (November 11, 1619) were to have a profound and lasting effect upon Descartes. He believed that this vision and the ensuing dreams had revealed to him his God-given vocation. They were to give him a much-needed confidence in his calling as well as in the correctness of its findings that was not always backed by argument. But for this experience, the brilliant dilettante might never have realized his vocation. It is ironic that Descartes, the great rationalist, should have found his inspiration in a mystical vision and highly irrational dreams. This element in Descartes's thinking is often overlooked in

French *lycées*, where the great Gallic hero and hypnophile is held up as a rationalist exemplar.

Descartes's dreams have attracted a wide variety of explanations. According to the Dutch philosopher and astronomer Huygens, who was later to correspond with Descartes, these dreams were the result of Descartes's brain becoming overheated while he was in the stove. Others have suggested indigestion, overwork, lack of sleep, a mystical crisis, or the fact that he might recently have joined the Rosicrucians. The melon, whose offstage existence is alluded to in the first dream, apparently caused much mirth to eighteenth-century readers of Descartes's biography. But with the advent of psychoanalysis, this melon became a much more serious matter.

As a result of his vision and the ensuing dreams, Descartes vowed that he would now dedicate his life to his intellectual studies, and would make a pilgrimage of thanksgiving to the shrine of Our Lady of Loretto in Italy. So it comes as rather a surprise when we learn that instead he continued drifting aimlessly about

Europe for another seven years (though he did manage to visit Loretto five years later). We have few precise details of Descartes's life during this seven-year period of "vagabond life," as he called it. To begin with, he seems to have joined the Imperial Hungarian army. But the Thirty Years War had now begun in earnest, and gentle-man-officer Descartes appears to have been none too keen for active campaigning. After leaving the army he traveled through France, Italy, Germany, Holland, Denmark, and Poland, all the time skillfully circumnavigating the regions where the war was being conducted by more dedicated members of his profession.

Not that Descartes was able to avoid violence altogether. While visiting one of the Frisian Islands (possibly Schiermonnikoog), he hired a boat to take him to the mainland. The sailors mistook him for a rich French merchant and planned to rob him along the way. As Descartes stood on deck watching the low island shoreline recede across the grey sea, the sailors working the ropes jabbered among themselves in Dutch, scheming how to hit him on the head, toss him overboard, and ransack the gold which they felt sure was hidden in his trunk. But their passenger had by now picked up a smattering of Dutch during his travels, and the hapless Schiermonnikoogers found themselves confronted by a dashing Descartes brandishing his sword. They quickly backed down, promising to transport him to the mainland in safety.

Sometime during this period, probably in 1623, Descartes returned home to La Haye and sold all his property. He then invested the cash in bonds, which were to provide him with a sound income for the rest of his life. One would think that during the course of this trip he might have stopped to see his family, but this is far from certain. Descartes never actually quarreled with his family, but he remained utterly detached from them. Despite his freedom to roam Europe at will, he didn't bother to return home for the weddings of his brother or his sister, and he did not even visit his father on his deathbed.

Toward the end of this period Descartes spent an increasing amount of time in Paris. Here he met an old school friend from La Flèche,

Marin Mersenne, who had joined the church. Father Mersenne had become a highly respected man of learning, in contact with the great minds of Europe. From Paris, Mersenne corresponded with such figures as Pascal, Fermat, and Gassendi. Mersenne's cell became a sort of clearinghouse for the latest ideas in mathematical, scientific, and philosophic thinking. This was just the kind of friend Descartes needed, and he was to correspond with Mersenne for the rest of his life, sending him manuscripts and testing his ideas on him both for their validity and to determine whether they conflicted with the teachings of the church.

Descartes spent most of his time in Paris closeted in his room studying. Occasionally friends would come round to discuss ideas with him; sometimes he was even persuaded out to more formal occasions. An anecdote relates how he was present at the residence of the papal nuncio when a certain Chandoux delivered a talk outlining "a new philosophy." At the end of the talk Descartes proceeded to dismember this new philosophy with the aid of some rigorous mathematical reasoning, to which Chandoux had no reply. After following Descartes's skillful arguments, Cardinal de Bérulle took him aside and strongly advised him to devote his life to philosophy.

For some reason this counsel appeared to win over Descartes. Visions and dreams may have inspired confidence in him, but it took the rational approach to urge him toward decisive action. In 1628 he retired to the north of France to live in seclusion and devote himself entirely to his thinking. Unfortunately his Parisian friends continued to visit him. So Descartes journeyed even farther afield and went to live in isolation in Holland, where he settled for more than two decades, until the year before his death.

But "settled" is very much a relative term where Descartes is concerned. During the first fifteen years of his residence in Holland he is known to have changed houses at least eighteen times. In between, when the settled domestic routine became all too much for him, he frequently traveled abroad. Only Father Mersenne could keep up with his address. This constant movement is put down to Descartes's love of solitude, but it seems to speak of some deeper restlessness. In the course of traveling, or even moving his home, one can't help meeting people even if only in passing fashion. This unending movement suggests that Descartes's solitude was not entirely self-sufficient. He was lonely but found it impossible to make contact with people except in the most trivial manner.

Descartes always had servants, and he appears to have cut quite a personable figure. The portraits we have of him depict a pale-faced gentleman in the dark flowing wig of the period; his mustachioed, drip-bearded features have a certain saturnine charm. He is said to have dressed well in fashionable knee breeches, black silk stockings, and silver buckle shoes. A silk scarf was always around his neck to protect it from the cold; and whenever he went out he wore a woolen scarf and heavy coat, and always put on his sword. He is said to have been sensitive to the slightest change of temperature, which he claimed affected the "inherited weakness" of his chest. Yet he spent years traveling throughout

Europe, from Italy to Scandinavia. And the country he finally chose to live in was Holland, notorious for its rain, fog, and ice, which a contemporary French visitor described as "four months of winter followed by eight months of cold." Or perhaps this was just the ideal spot for a dedicated hypochondriac.

But Holland had one great advantage: in the seventeenth century it was the duty-free zone of the European mind. Unlike in other nations, here you didn't have to pay for your ideas. The tolerant Dutch had dispensed with such heavy-duty items as the Inquisition, heresy, the rack, and burning at the stake—critical accolades that greeted original thinkers elsewhere in Europe. Of the four great thinkers who produced original philosophy during the seventeenth century, no less than three—Descartes, Spinoza, and Locke —lived for periods in Holland. (The other, Leibniz, lived across the border in Hannover, and visited Holland several times.) Partly as a result of this liberal atmosphere, Holland also became a thriving center of the printing industry, with works by such advanced thinkers as Galileo and

Hobbes being published here. It was a time when new ideas thrived in Holland as nowhere else in Europe.

Descartes began this productive period of his life with high hopes. As a result of his vision in the Bavarian stove, he had conceived of a universal science capable of embracing all human knowledge. This would arrive at truth by the use of reason. But this was much more than just a revolutionary new method. (Reason had played very much a backseat role in the sciences and alchemies of the Middle Ages.) Descartes had conceived of a system that would not only include all knowledge but also unite it. This system would be free from prejudices and assumptions, and would be based on certainty alone. It would start from basic principles, which were themselves self-evident, and would build from these.

Descartes foresaw immense advantages from his system. He confidently predicted that when this new scientific method was applied to medicine it would be able to slow the aging process. (This was Descartes's persistent dream. Ten years later he wrote to the Dutch scholar Huygens that, despite his parlous physical condition, he expected to live until he was well over one hundred, though in the last decade of his life he revised this estimate downward by a few years.)

Descartes began writing a treatise that he called Rules for the Direction of the Mind. In order to discover the universal science, he argued, we first had to adopt a method of thinking properly. This method consisted of following two rules of mental operation: intuition and deduction. Intuition Descartes defined as "the conception, without doubt, of an unclouded and attentive mind, which is formed by the light of reason alone." Deduction was defined as "necessary inference from other facts which are known for certain." Descartes's celebrated method—which came to be known as the Cartesian Method—lay in the correct application of these two rules of thought.

Descartes was now gaining a reputation as a thinker on a wide range of philosophical and scientific subjects. In March 1629 the pope and certain senior cardinals began observing UFOs in the sky above Rome. As the sun set, a solar halo would appear with orbiting spots of brilliant light. Letters were sent to Descartes and various other leading thinkers, asking their opinion of these visions.

Descartes was so intrigued that for a time he gave up his philosophical thinking to concentrate on this matter. He had his suspicions about the cause of such phenomena but refused to commit himself until several years later. By this time he had completed an entire treatise on the subject. (Meanwhile, one Vatican source had offered its own explanation: the phenomena were caused by angels undertaking celestial scene-changes in preparation for the Second Coming.) Descartes suggested that these lights in the sky were caused by meteors. Unfortunately modern scientists have an explanation that sounds even more implausible than the Vatican's. These phenomena, now called parhelia, are said to be caused when the sun shines "through a thin cloud composed of hexagonal ice crystals falling with their principal axes vertical." Crystals performing formation dances in the atmosphere are now considered much more likely than angels, and simplistic explanations such as Descartes's are laughed out of court.

In this as in many other matters, Descartes was alive during a brief and possibly unique era of human thought. The new explanations put forward by the finest scientific and philosophical minds of his time were in many cases both plausible and comprehensible. They also tended to be rational and, in their overall conception, simple—with the aim of leaving space for the contemplation of ultimate mysteries. Humanity is unlikely to experience such an era again. Afterward it would become increasingly impossible to understand the truth, except in the narrowing field that one was capable of understanding. From now on we were to know more and more about less and less.

Having laid down his rules for the working of the mind, Descartes now set about the outer world. For the next three years he composed a Treatise on the Universe. This contained his ideas on an enormous range of scientific subjects, including meteors, dioptrics, and geometry. In order to pursue his studies in anatomy he now took to visiting the local slaughterhouse, returning home with various specimens hidden under his cloak so that he could dissect them in private. As a result of this work, Descartes originated the study of embryology. (According to legend, on one of these visits to the abattoir Descartes noticed a portly young man sketching the flayed carcass of an ox, and asked him why he had chosen such a subject. "Your philosophy takes away our souls," replied the artist. "In my paintings I will give them back, even to dead animals." The young artist is said to have been Rembrandt.)

After three years of concentrated work, Descartes prepared to send the manuscript of his Treatise on the Universe to Father Mersenne, for publication in Paris. Then, like a bolt from the blue, fantastic news arrived from Rome: Galileo had been charged with heresy, brought before the Inquisition, and forced to swear that he "abjured, cursed, and detested" his scientific works. Most specifically this referred to his belief in Copernicus's theory that the earth moved around the sun. Descartes immediately asked his friend Beeckman for a copy of Galileo's work, and found to his dismay that many of Galileo's conclusions were identical to his own. Without a word to anyone, Descartes put away his Treatise on the Universe and turned his thoughts to less controversial matters. The work was not published until years after Descartes's death, and then only in part.

Descartes's life was riven by dichotomies. He longed for peace and solitude, yet his loneliness drove him to obsessive travel. As a daringly original thinker he vowed to "follow my thoughts wherever they might lead"; yet as a man he swore "to obey the laws of my country, adhere to the religion of my fathers, and follow the example of the wisest men I meet." He was convinced that what he had written in his Treatise on the Universe was correct, yet he also firmly believed in the God of the church. Descartes has been accused of cowardice, of being a secret atheist, and of not even knowing himself despite all his introspective meditations. None of these accusations stand. Descartes may not have been of the stuff of martyrs, but that doesn't make him a coward. He was convinced that without dropping any of its Scholastic tenets the church could still come round to his point of view. And his intellectual self-knowledge was deeper than that of any philosopher since Socrates, even if it did contain a few psychological blind spots.

Yet the greatest dichotomy that beset Descartes lay in his philosophy. Descartes saw the world as consisting of two kinds of substance, mind and matter. Mind was unextended and indivisible. Matter was extended and divisible, and obeyed the laws of physics. This meant that our incorporeal mind was lodged in a mechanistic body. But how could the mind, which had no extension, interact with a body which could only obey the mechanistic laws of science? Descartes never satisfactorily solved this problem, which so uncannily echoes the psychological dichotomies that beset him in daily life. Yet he did try to produce an answer. According to Descartes, the mind and the body interact in the pineal gland (an obscure organ near the base of the brain, whose precise function remains uncertain to this day). Unfortunately Descartes rather missed the point here. The question was not so much where they interact but how.

A rare human element now enters Descartes's life: he has an affair with a girl named Helene, who may have been one of his servants. As a result he has a daughter whom he calls Francine. After the birth of Francine, Helene lives with her daughter in a nearby house but visits him regularly. When others are present, Descartes passes off Francine as his niece.

From these few facts it is difficult to know for certain what kind of relationship he had with Helene. But it's easy enough to conjecture. Poor Helene—what did she make of this upper-class cold fish with the emotional range of a fileted cod? What did she register when she gazed into those shadow-ringed abstracted eyes of his? Helene may not have been able to break through to Descartes, but Francine certainly did. Guilelessly she reached out to him, and he responded. (It wasn't so much that he'd been rejected in his childhood: there was just no one there, except old nanny with her potato love.) Despite attempting to pass Francine off as his niece, Descartes soon grew to love his little daughter, and she offered him a unique emotional experience in his life.

He was now writing what is today considered his most original work, his *Discourse on Method*. Ironically the body of this book consisted of safer portions lifted from his Treatise on the Universe. These contained ideas that were to change the face of mathematics and make several revolutionary advances in science. In this work Descartes laid the foundations of modern analytic geometry and introduced coordinates (later to be named Cartesian coordinates by Leibniz); in optics he proposed the Law of Diffraction and put forward an explanation of the rainbow; and he attempted a rational scientific theory to explain the weather (which, like our present theories, ended up only working retrospectively). But far and away the most important part of the *Discourse on Method* is the comparatively brief introduction. This outlines the thinking that was to change the course of philosophy.

And in an even more revolutionary departure from tradition, Descartes makes these ideas both comprehensible and readable.

How is it possible to convey profoundly original philosophical insights with sufficient clarity so that anyone can understand them? This problem has defeated most of the great minds of philosophy. Plato cracked it by setting out his philosophy in the form of dinner-party conversations. Nietzsche thought he'd cracked it by writing the most brilliant, subtle, and powerful prose ever penned in German, but his megalomania turned into pure mania. Wittgenstein attempted to circumvent the problem by allowing for the attention span of the TV age and writing brilliant two-line remarks; but he refused to back them up with philosophic argument. Descartes succeeded in overcoming this problem by the simplest and most obvious method of all. In clear autobiographical prose he describes how he goes about his thinking, and the thoughts that occur to him in the process. When you read Descartes you experience what it is like to be a great mind thinking original philosophy. And he describes this so deceptively well that you think it's easy. It appears no different from the way you might think. Step by rational step you follow him to his conclusion.

Descartes begins by taking the reader back to snow-covered Bavaria and the time of his vision. "Winter set in, and I found myself in a spot where there was no society of any interest. At the time I was unworried by any cares or passions, so I took to spending my day in a stove, where I could be alone with my thoughts." In surprisingly cool prose he then goes on to describe how it is possible, by means of persistent and determined doubt, for us to destroy our belief in the entire fabric of the world around us. Nothing remains certain. The whole universe, our very individuality, even our own existence may all be a dream. We have no way of knowing anything for certain. Except for one thing. No matter how deluded I may be in my thoughts about myself and the world, there is just one thing that is undeniable: I am thinking. This alone proves to me my existence. In the most famous remark in philosophy, Descartes concludes: "*Cogito ergo sum*" (I think, therefore I am).

Having established his one ultimate certainty, Descartes proceeds to rebuild upon this foundation all that he has doubted. The world, the truths of mathematics, the snowbound Bavarian winter—all return with cold certainty, chastened by their period of banishment to the never-never land of doubt, but more indubitable than ever now that they are built on such an indubitable foundation.

Having had the courage to doubt the entire universe, Descartes typically chose to publish his work anonymously. He also published it in French, in the hope of reaching a wider audience. He wished to avoid controversy with the church and hoped to do so by appealing to people who were interested in the new sciences. Astonishingly, this almost worked. Almost. People soon determined the author of *Discourse on Method*, but at first they were more interested in its mathematical and scientific theories. Descartes revolutionized the field of optics by discovering the law of refraction. But his advances in geometry were even more revolutionary. Here he introduced the notion of coordinates (to this day known as Cartesian coordinates, after him). These enabled the identification of a fixed point by reference to a horizontal and a vertical plane. He also introduced algebra to solve geometric problems, thus founding analytic geometry. Mathematicians were fascinated, then outraged.

For most of us, the one certain thing about mathematics is that it's either correct or incorrect. Such a naive approach immediately disqualifies one from the realm of true mathematicians. Having read Descartes's new mathematical theories and recognized their profound originality, all the great mathematicians of the era were soon gunning for him. Gassendi, Pascal, Insen, Fermat . . . one by one they entered the fray.

Such controversies are well beyond the comprehension of mere mortals. Those who believe otherwise may find the old story of Fermat's Last Theorem instructive. According to this, there are no whole numbers above two, such that the following expression is true:

$$X^n + Y^n = Z^n$$

Shortly before Fermat died he wrote in the margin beside this formula: "I have discovered a truly remarkable proof for this, but there's no room to write it down here." Despite repeated attempts by many of the finest mathematical minds of the past three centuries, not until the 1990s has someone at last managed to find a proof for Fermat's Last Theorem. Even this has been disputed. For centuries many mathematicians maintained that Fermat's Last Theorem couldn't possibly be true, others that it must be. Some are convinced that Fermat was bluffing, still others that he didn't dare try to prove it. Mathematics begins in certainty and ends like this.

Philosophy, on the other hand, both begins and ends like this. When someone is described as having a philosophical attitude, you can be sure he's not a philosopher. This Descartes quickly discovered. After the mathematicians, it was the philosophers' turn to attack him. In no time Descartes found himself in trouble with the church. If you could doubt everything except the fact that you were thinking, where did this leave God? Fortunately Descartes's friends rallied to defend him, and, even more fortunately, Descartes was living in Holland.

Or rather, moving in Holland. In 1638, for the fifteenth time since taking up residence in the Netherlands, Descartes moved his home once again, this time to Amersfoort, just outside the ancient university city of Utrecht. By now his daughter Francine was five years old, and he was planning to send her to France so that she could become "a fine lady." Suddenly Francine took ill and died. Descartes was devastated. It was the most bitter blow he was to suffer in his lifetime, and according to his biographer Baillet "he wept for his child with a tenderness which showed that the thought of eternity is capable of being extinguished by the grief of the moment."

This tragedy occurred while Descartes was finishing his *Meditations*, generally considered his masterpiece. Although not as immediately appealing as the *Discourse on Method*, it is graced with the same felicity of style, and its French is a model expression of abstract thought.

(Descartes gallantly claimed that he had written it with the aim of making abstract ideas exciting to women.) This time he took the precaution of sending the manuscript to Father Mersenne in Paris and asking him to circulate it so that he might discover "the opinions of the learned." Descartes wished to have the approval of the scholars and the Jesuits for his new philosophical treatise which contained an elaboration of the ideas put forward in the *Discourse on Method*. This time he proposes an even more comprehensive program of doubt. He imagines that the entire universe, even the truths of geometry and the winter dressing gown he is wearing as he sits in front of the fire, may be the work of a malignant unseen being intent on deceiving him. (Psychologists have confidently identified the antihero of this fantasy as Judge Joachim Descartes.) Once again the doubtful workings of Descartes's mind arrive at the same indisputable cog. And upon this self-evident principle of ultimate certainty he once again rebuilds the universe, even going as far as to prove the existence of God with arguments first used by St. Anselm and Thomas Aquinas more than four centuries earlier, presumably in order to make the church feel more comfortable.

Although this process of Cartesian doubt was not strictly original, it was considered as such at the time. St. Augustine's remarkably similar doubts and conclusion, put forward twelve centuries earlier, were not central to his thought and had been completely ignored. But more recently, and more interestingly, the Portuguese philosopher Francisco Sanches had proposed almost the exact same program of comprehensive doubt in his astonishing treatise *Quod Nihil Sicitur* (*Why Nothing Can Be Known*). This had been published sixty years before Descartes's *Meditations*, in 1581. Fortunately for Sanches, his treatise attracted little attention, otherwise he might have ended as a great philosophic martyr at the age of thirty-one.

Descartes had no ambitions for martyrdom, and though he possessed many of the qualifications for obscurity (under other circumstances, his sloth alone would surely have qualified him), he appears to have had no ambitions in this direction either. He wanted to be heard, but he also wanted to be accepted. He was utterly convinced that he was right, but he wanted the church to be convinced too. So under his instructions Father Mersenne sent the manuscript of the *Meditations* to such luminaries of the European intellectual scene as Gassendi, Hobbes, and Arnauld. And they replied, putting forward their objections to Descartes's theories. These objections irritated Descartes, but he was persuaded to add his replies, and the *Meditations* were finally published in 1641, complete with objections and Descartes's rebuttals.

Inevitably the publication of Descartes's *Meditations* provoked an even worse furor. The Jesuits correctly realized that Cartesian doubt and *Cogito ergo sum* spelled the end of Scholastic philosophy and Aquinas. Worse still for Descartes, this time the controversy spilled over into Holland. The president of the University of Utrecht accused Descartes of atheism. Ingeniously he likened Descartes to Vanini, who had been charged with purposely putting forward weak and ineffectual proofs of the existence of

God. (Vanini had been burned at the stake in 1619 in Toulouse.) Even more damaging attacks came from other important Dutch figures, accusing him of heresy. In those days atheism was one thing, but heresy was a matter of mortal consequences. Fortunately the French ambassador intervened on Descartes's behalf, and eventually the controversy waned, though for some time afterward Descartes's name and works were not allowed to be mentioned within the precincts of the University of Utrecht. Ultimately this ban was dropped after the mathematics department complained that they were unable to do geometry without making use of Cartesian coordinates.

Descartes was now renowned throughout Europe, his fame stretching so far beyond the intellectual world that he was read even by royalty. When the young Queen Christina of Sweden encountered one of his books she was so impressed that she invited him to court. He must come to Stockholm and teach her philosophy. By now the long hard years of late rising and gentlemanly meditation were beginning to take their toll on Descartes. Although only fifty-three, he hadn't moved his home for four years. He was now living on a small estate at Egmund-Binnen, twenty miles north of Amsterdam near the sea. He did his meditations sitting in his octagonal study looking out over a beautiful old garden. Occasionally he would travel to Paris, where he discussed his ideas with old sparring partners like Gassendi, Pascal, Hobbes, and Arnauld.

The prospect of a long trip north to Sweden did not appeal. But Queen Christina was a headstrong and determined woman. Only twenty-three years old, she had already made her mark on her kingdom. Just five feet tall, she had broad shoulders and trained like a soldier. It was said that she could gallop for more than ten hours without tiring (though one wonders about the horse). When she ascended to the throne she vowed to turn her capital, the watery Venice of the North, into the intellectual Paris of the North. Despite her determined efforts, it remained undeniably the Stockholm of the North. Descartes was her big chance, and she was determined not to let him slip from her grasp. To reinforce her invitation she sent an admiral and a warship to collect him. But Descartes caviled, albeit in most gallant fashion, handing to the waiting admiral a flattering missive describing how "Her Majesty was created in the image of God to a greater degree than the rest of mankind," but prayed to be excused from "basking in the sunbeams of her glorious presence."

Christina stamped her foot, the court had a bad day, and another ship was dispatched to fetch the immobile philosopher. Descartes, who had defeated the finest minds of Europe in intellectual argument, was forced to concede defeat. In October 1649 he sailed for Stockholm. There he was welcomed by the queen and had two personal audiences with her. Christina appeared to have absorbed little philosophy from the study of his works; and then she found she had other matters to attend to. Descartes was left to amuse himself for six seeks while the bitter Swedish winter set in. (It was to be the worst for sixty years: the city icebound for six months, gloom at noon, and beyond the suburbs the wolves howling in the frigid blast beneath the aurora borealis.) Midway through January, when Christina decided it was time she started her philosophy lessons, Descartes was duly summoned. The queen, he was informed, would have three philosophy lessons a week, each starting at 5 a.m.

Even in the army Descartes had never risen before 11 a.m. The shock of rising at 4 a.m. in deepest Scandinavian winter, attending to his toilet with French fastidiousness during the Hour of the Wolf, followed by a fast, bumpy sleigh ride over the iron-iced streets through the piercing Arctic blast—there's no point in even trying to imagine how he felt. Within two weeks he caught a chill, which soon turned into pneumonia. A week later he became delirious, and on February 11, 1650, he died. One of the great minds of Europe had been sacrificed to the whim of royalty. As a Catholic in Protestant Sweden, this deeply religious man could not be buried in sacred ground but had to be interred in the cemetery for unbaptized children.

Thirteen years later the Catholic church honored Descartes's memory by placing all his works on its Index of Banned Books (a tradition that continues to this day, when Plato's *Sympo-*

sium was recently put on the index in Ireland). Later in the seventeenth century Descartes's body was transferred to Paris where it was reinterred. During the Revolution a proposal was put forward that he should be exhumed again and placed in the Pantheon, alongside other great French thinkers. This was put to the National Assembly. In an unusual move, the members divided along scientific lines. Those who favored the mechanistic Cartesian view of the universe were opposed by members who supported the new Newtonian theory of gravity.

Descartes had proposed the Theory of Vortices to explain how the universe worked. His theory maintained that the movement of one particle affected the movement of all other particles throughout the universe. This took place through a series of interlocking vortices, which encompassed everything from the solar system and the stars down to the smallest particles. This would of course have resulted in a system of fiendish complexity, such as only a mathematician could conceive. Yet it points to a matter of some interest in the evolution of human thought.

Descartes's theory bears a passing resemblance both to the double helix of DNA and the Superstring Theory of ultimate particles. Also, in his long search for a force that could interact between mind and body, Descartes was looking for something similar to radio waves or electricity. According to the modern thinker Jean de Mandeville, this points to the possibility that human understanding evolves along certain conceptual lines almost regardless of its object.

In the vote in the French National Assembly, the Newtonians managed to muster sufficient support to defeat the Cartesians. Gravity had won the day. Descartes would have to be buried elsewhere.

Formerly the truth had been the province of theology, now it had entered the realm of democracy. Descartes didn't fit into either. Appropriately he is now buried in the Church of St. Germain des Pres, in the heart of the Latin Quarter in Paris, where his tradition of doubtful thinking and noon rising is staunchly maintained to this day.

Afterword

Descartes brought philosophy back to life. His revolutionary new way of thinking about the world, and our status in it, gradually transformed European thought. Things would never be the same again. He instigated a widespread rejection of the moribund Aristotelianism that had gained such a stranglehold on the European mind. From this time on, Aristotelianism was no longer taken seriously by the leading philosophers of the day, though its deathly influence lingered on in universities and seminaries for years to come.

This residue was not entirely to philosophy's

detriment. The next generations of philosophers—including Leibniz, Locke, Berkeley, and Hume—all had to endure an Aristotelian education. This stupefying experience inspired each of them. Philosophy just couldn't go on like this—and instead they decided to think for themselves. Each in turn began looking for an alternative method of thought, and each in turn discovered Descartes. Being genuine philosophers, they soon found objections to this new philosophy. (No great philosopher worthy of the calling ever accepts the thought of his predecessors without question. For him there can be only one incontrovertible way of thinking—his own.)

As a result, these new philosophers each set about constructing their own incontrovertible explanation of the world and its problems. Yet all these thinkers, whether they reject or develop Descartes's ideas, stand in his debt.

With Descartes, the primacy of the individual and the analysis of human consciousness became fundamental to philosophy. Emphasis was also placed on reason rather than dogma. From now on problems could be approached from a reasonable point of view. Solutions that didn't square with teachings founded on the experiences of a resourceful Bronze Age tribe, or the ideas of a Balkan wise man who had died almost two thousand years earlier, were not necessarily dismissed out of hand.

As with all such revolutionary figures, Descartes attracted his inevitable band of followers. They developed his ideas into the philosophy that became known as Cartesianism. And it was now that the shortcomings of Descartes's philosophy became exposed.

Descartes insisted on the rational approach: the problems of philosophy could be solved by analyzing them with the use of reason alone. His famous all-embracing process of doubt left this as the only certain evidence. Doubting the evidence of the senses led him to deny experience as a source of certain knowledge. (Here, for once, Aristotle remained right: science could only be based on experience.) In Descartes's view the universe was entirely mechanistic. The physical and biological aspects of the world all worked like a machine, and its innermost mechanics could thus—in theory at least—all be calculated. Belief in this approach remains to this day. Not only is the assessment of subnuclear particles largely a matter of calculation, but we believe that the answers *must* be susceptible to calculation.

Descartes's negation of experience as a certain source of knowledge was soon to prove an embarrassment. Europe was now entering a great age of scientific discovery, which was to reach a peak in Newton's conception of universal gravity. The advances made during this period—from Harvey's discovery of the circulation of the blood to Halley's discovery of his comet—depended almost exclusively upon observation.

At the same time philosophy too rejected Descartes. The British thinkers Locke, Berkeley, and Hume turned to empiricism: the belief in the primacy of experience as the source of our knowledge.

Yet Cartesianism was not entirely exploded. The Cartesians included some colorful figures, and a number became champions of the scientific revolution. The Parisian Régis conducted sensational demonstrations of the new Cartesian physics at his public lectures, which became so popular that they were closed down by Louis XIV as a danger to public order. Descartes's best-known follower was the French priest Malebranche, who became so convinced of Descartes's mechanistic ideas that he believed in kicking dogs to demonstrate that they were nothing but machines with utterly predictable responses (boot, bark). Malebranche acknowledged that Descartes had failed to explain the interaction of mind and body, but he put forward the theory of Occasionalism to overcome this gap. According to Malebranche, the mind and the body occupy two entirely separate worlds which never interact and are incapable of affecting each other. But what happens when the mind wills the foot to move, and it then kicks the dog? On every occasion when the mind wills something in its separate mental world, Malebranche explained, God arranges for the material world to undergo a parallel adjustment. There is no such thing as cause and effect, just two separate parallel worlds. According to Occasionalism, these two worlds act in concert on all occasions through the agency of God. The ingenuity of the new science still had a long way to go before it could match the ingenuity of the old theology.

Descartes's last notable follower was the eighteenth-century philosopher La Mettrie. He took the logical step of dismissing the mental world and insisting upon a purely mechanistic materialism, with no place for parallel universes or even for God. La Mettrie ended up as court philosopher to Frederick the Great, where he found it prudent to keep quiet about his atheism. But it was an overenthusiastic demonstration of his thoroughgoing materialism that eventually led to his demise. He died after consuming a surfeit of pheasant paté, attempting to prove the mechanics of the digestive system to fellow court intellectuals.

Descartes's insistence on the primacy of the individual, and the analysis of human consciousness, were to prove his most lasting legacies. Both rationalism and the opposing empiricism agreed upon the need for such an emphasis. And in one form or another this attitude continued to dominate philosophy until comparatively recently. Only with the arrival of logical analysis was the primacy of the individual and the analysis of human consciousness superseded by the primacy of the dictionary and the analysis of its contents. Once more, philosophy stands in need of a Descartes to bring it back to life.

From Descartes's Writings

It is some time since I first realized how many false opinions I accepted as true from my childhood, and how doubtful was the entire structure of thought which I had built upon them. I therefore understood that I must, if I wanted to establish anything at all in science that was firm and liable to last, once and for all rid myself of all the opinions I had adopted, and start from an entirely new foundation.

—*Meditations*, I

A multitude of laws often hampers justice, so that a state is best governed when it has only a few laws which are strictly administered; similarly, instead of the large number of laws which make up logic, I was of the opinion that the four following laws were perfectly sufficient for me, provided I took the firm and unwavering resolution to stick to them clearly at all times.

The first was never to accept anything as true if I did not clearly know it to be so; that is, carefully to avoid precipitate conclusions and preconceptions, and to include nothing more in my judgment than was presented clearly and distinctly to my mind, so that I had no reason to doubt it.

The second, to divide each of the difficulties I examined into as many parts as possible, and as might be necessary for a proper solution.

The third, to conduct my thoughts in an orderly fashion, by starting with the simplest and most easily known objects, so that I could ascend, little by little, and step by step, to more complex knowledge; and by giving some order even to those objects which appeared to have none.

And the last, always to make enumerations

so complete, and reviews so comprehensive, that I could be sure of leaving nothing out.

—*Discourse on Method,* Part I

The long chains of simple and easy reasonings, which geometers use to reach the most difficult conclusions, had given me reason to suppose that all things which can be known by humanity are connected in some way. And that there is nothing so far removed from us as to be beyond our reach, or so hidden that we cannot discover it, as long as we abstain from accepting the false for the true, and always preserve in our thoughts the order necessary for the deduction of one truth from another. Also, I had little difficulty in determining the objects with which it was necessary to commence, for I was already convinced that these must be the simplest and easiest known.

—*Discourse on Method,* Part II

Since I desired to devote myself wholly to the search for truth, I thought it necessary . . . to reject as if utterly false anything in which I could discover the least grounds for doubt, so that I could find out if I was left with anything at all which was absolutely indubitable. Thus, because our senses sometimes deceive us, I decided to suppose that nothing was really as they led us to believe it was. And, because some of us make mistakes in reasoning, committing logical errors in even the simplest matters of geometry, I rejected as erroneous all reasonings that I had previously taken as proofs. And finally, when I considered that the very same things we perceive when we are awake may also occur to us while we are asleep and not perceiving anything at all, I resolved to pretend that anything that had ever entered my mind was no more than a dream. But immediately I noticed that while I was thinking in this way, and regarding everything as false, it was nonetheless absolutely necessary that I, who was doing this thinking, was still something. And observing that this truth, "I think, therefore I am," was so sure and certain that no ground for doubt, be it ever so extravagantly skeptical, was capable of shaking it, I therefore decided that I could accept it without scruple as the first principle of the philosophy I was seeking to create.

—Discourse on Method, Part IV

There is a vast difference between the mind and the body, in that the body by its very nature is always divisible, while the mind is completely indivisible. For when I consider the mind, or rather when I consider myself simply as a thinking thing, I find I can distinguish no parts within myself, and I clearly discern that I am a thing utterly one and complete. Although my whole mind seems to be united to my whole body, when a foot, or an arm, or any other part is severed, I am not conscious of anything having been removed from my mind. Nor can the faculties of willing, perceiving, conceptualizing, and so forth, in any way be called parts of the mind, as it is always the same mind which is doing the willing, perceiving, conceptualizing, and so forth.

Meanwhile, utterly the opposite holds for all corporeal or extended things. For I cannot imagine any one of them which I cannot in my thoughts easily split into parts, and thus I understand that it is divisible.

—*Meditations*, 6

Good sense is most evenly distributed among all humanity; for all consider themselves to be so well endowed with it that even those who complain of their lot in all other ways seldom express the desire for more good sense. And here it is unlikely that everyone is mistaken. It shows rather that the power of correct judgment and the ability to distinguish truth from error—what we properly call good sense or reason—is by nature equally given to all humanity. As a result, the diversity of our opinions does not arise from any of us being endowed with a greater quantity of reason, but solely because we direct our thoughts in different directions and do not pay attention to the same things. For it is not enough just to have a fine mind; the main thing is to learn how to apply it properly. The finest minds are capable of both the greatest vices as well as the greatest virtues; and those who travel slowly often make better progress, as long as they follow the right path, than those who rush ahead and stray from it.

—*Discourse on Method*, Part I

The nature of clear and distinct perception: There are some people who throughout their entire lives perceive nothing in the correct fashion so as to be capable of judging it properly. The knowledge upon which a certain and incontrovertible judgment can be based must not only be clear but also distinct. Whatever is present and apparent to an attentive mind I call clear—in the same fashion as we assert that we see objects clearly when they are present to our gazing eye and make a strong impression upon it. But a thing that is distinct is so precise and different from all other objects that it contains within itself nothing else but what is clear.

—*Principles of Philosophy*, Principle XLV

Chronology of Significant Philosophical Dates

6th C B.C.	The beginning of Western philosophy with Thales of Miletus.
End of 6th C B.C.	Death of Pythagoras.
399 B.C.	Socrates sentenced to death in Athens.
c 387 B.C.	Plato founds the Academy in Athens, the first university.
335 B.C.	Aristotle founds the Lyceum in Athens, a rival school to the Academy.

324 A.D.	Emperor Constantine moves capital of Roman Empire to Byzantium.
400 A.D.	St. Augustine writes his *Confessions*. Philosophy absorbed into Christian theology.
410 A.D.	Sack of Rome by Visigoths heralds opening of Dark Ages.
529 A.D.	Closure of Academy in Athens by Emperor Justinian marks end of Hellenic thought.
Mid-13th C	Thomas Aquinas writes his commentaries on Aristotle. Era of Scholasticism.
1453	Fall of Byzantium to Turks, end of Byzantine Empire.
1492	Columbus reaches America. Renaissance in Florence and revival of interest in Greek learning.
1543	Copernicus publishes *On the Revolution of the Celestial Orbs*, proving mathematically that the earth revolves around the sun.

1633	Galileo forced by church to recant heliocentric theory of the universe.
1641	Descartes publishes his *Meditations*, the start of modern philosophy.
1677	Death of Spinoza allows publication of his *Ethics*.
1687	Newton publishes *Principia*, introducing concept of gravity.
1689	Locke publishes *Essay Concerning Human Understanding*. Start of empiricism.
1710	Berkeley publishes *Principles of Human Knowledge*, advancing empiricism to new extremes.
1716	Death of Leibniz.
1739–1740	Hume publishes *Treatise of Human Nature*, taking empiricism to its logical limits.
1781	Kant, awakened from his "dogmatic slumbers" by Hume, publishes *Critique of Pure Reason*.

	Great era of German metaphysics begins.
1807	Hegel publishes *The Phenomenology of Mind*, high point of German metaphysics.
1818	Schopenhauer publishes *The World as Will and Representation*, introducing Indian philosophy into German metaphysics.
1889	Nietzsche, having declared "God is dead," succumbs to madness in Turin.
1921	Wittgenstein publishes *Tractatus Logico-Philosophicus*, claiming the "final solution" to the problems of philosophy.
1920s	Vienna Circle propounds Logical Positivism.
1927	Heidegger publishes *Being and Time*, heralding split between analytical and Continental philosophy.
1943	Sartre publishes *Being and Nothingness*, advancing

Heidegger's thought and instigating existentialism.

1953   Posthumous publication of Wittgenstein's *Philosophical Investigations*. High era of linguistic analysis.

Chronology of Descartes's Life

1596	René Descartes born March 31.
1606	Enters Jesuit College at La Flèche.
1614–1616	Studies for law degree at Poitiers.
1618	Joins army of the Prince of Orange in Holland; meets physicist Beeckman.
1619–1628	Travels through Europe "studying from the book of the world."
1619	Has dreams which convince him to dedicate his life to thought.
1620	Conceives of his universal method in a stove in Bavaria.

1622–1624	Moves to Paris; meets Father Mersenne, who is in correspondence with many of the great minds of Europe.
1628	Moves to the Netherlands.
1633	Writes *Le Monde* (*The World*) but suppresses publication after the church condemns Galileo.
1635	Birth of Descartes's daughter, Francine.
1637	Publishes *Discourse on Method*.
1640	Death of his daughter causes Descartes profound grief.
1641	Publishes *Meditations on the First Philosophy*, which contains his famous assertion "*Cogito, ergo sum*" (I think, therefore I am).
1648	Death of his friend Father Mersenne in Paris.
1649	Travels to court of Queen Christina in Sweden.
1650	Dies in Stockholm on February 11.

Chronology of Descartes's Era

1598	Edict of Nantes grants toleration to Huguenots (French Protestants).
1599	Birth of Velásquez.
1600	Population of Europe reaches 100 million, having doubled in previous 150 years.
1600s	French begin settling Canada.
1605	Francis Bacon publishes *Advancement of Learning*, which proposes scientific method in place of Aristotelianism.
1607	Founding of Jamestown in America.

1609	Founding of Bank of Amsterdam breaks monopoly of private banking families.
1616	Death of Cervantes; death of Shakespeare.
1618	Start of the Thirty Years War, which spreads through Europe.
1620	Pilgrim Fathers reach Cape Cod.
1621	United Provinces of the Netherlands at war with Spain.
1624	French *parlement* passes decree forbidding attacks on Aristotle on pain of death.
1628	Harvey publishes work describing circulation of the blood.
1629	Peace after religious wars in France.
1639	Birth of Racine.
1642	Death of Galileo; birth of Newton.
1646	Birth of Leibniz.
1648	End of Thirty Years War, leaving large parts of Europe (especially Germany) devastated.

1649   Revolution in England deposes
Charles I.

Recommended Reading

John G. Cottingham, ed., *The Cambridge Companion to Descartes* (Cambridge University Press, 1992)

Tom Sorell, *Descartes* (Oxford University Press, 1987)

Stanley Tweyman, ed., *René Descartes' Meditations on First Philosophy in Focus* (Routledge, 1993)

Bernard Williams, *Descartes: The Project of Pure Enquiry* (Viking Penguin, 1990)

Margaret Dauler Wilson, *Descartes* (Routledge, 1978)

Index

87

A NOTE ON THE AUTHOR

Paul Strathern has lectured in philosophy and mathematics and now lives and writes in London. A Somerset Maugham prize winner, he is also the author of books on history and travel as well as five novels. His articles have appeared in a great many publications, including the *Observer* (London) and the *Irish Times*. His own degree in philosophy was earned at Trinity College, Dublin.